French Apple Cake Cookbook

A Delectable Journey Through the Flavors of French Apple Cakes

While every precaution has been taken in the preparation of this book, the publisher assumes no responsibility for errors or omissions, or for damages resulting from the use of the information contained herein.

FRENCH APPLE CAKE COOKBOOK

First edition. November 1, 2023.

Copyright © 2023 Sammy Andrews.

ISBN: 979-8223207702

Written by Sammy Andrews.

Sammy Andrews

Introduction to French Apple Cakes

- The History of French Apple Cakes
- Regional Variations
- Why French Apple Cakes are Special
- Ingredients Overview

Essential Tools and Ingredients

- Must-Have Kitchen Equipment
- Selecting the Perfect Apples
- Flour and Other Dry Ingredients
- Dairy and Non-Dairy Options

Classic French Apple Cake

- Recipe: Traditional French Apple Cake
- Step-by-Step Instructions
- Tips for a Perfectly Moist Cake
- Serving Suggestions

Normandy Apple Cake

- The Charm of Normandy
- Recipe: Normandy Apple Cake
- A Taste of Calvados
- Garnishing Ideas

Tarte Tatin: A French Apple Upside-Down Cake

- The Story Behind Tarte Tatin
- Recipe: Tarte Tatin
- Flipping Techniques
- Pairing with Vanilla Ice Cream

Breton Apple Cake: Far Breton aux Pommes

- Breton Culinary Traditions
- Recipe: Far Breton aux Pommes
- Unique Texture of Far
- Whiskey or Rum Additions

Apple and Calvados Cake

- A Toast to Calvados
- Recipe: Apple and Calvados Cake
- Aromatic Calvados Glaze
- Serving in Style

Rustic French Apple Galette

- Rustic Elegance in a Galette
- Recipe: Rustic French Apple Galette
- Folded Pastry Technique
- Perfect Galette Presentation

Apple and Cinnamon Clafoutis

- Clafoutis: Beyond Cherries
- Recipe: Apple and Cinnamon Clafoutis
- Spice Variations
- A Dusting of Powdered Sugar

Alsace-Style Apple Kugelhopf

- The Alsace Region's Influence
- Recipe: Alsace-Style Apple Kugelhopf
- Rich Almond Filling
- A Crown of Slivered Almonds

Savory Apple and Brie Tart

- Savory Side of French Apple Cakes
- Recipe: Savory Apple and Brie Tart
- Cheese Pairings
- Fresh Herb Garnish

Provencal Olive Oil Apple Cake

- Mediterranean Flavors in a Cake
- Recipe: Provencal Olive Oil Apple Cake
- Olive Oil Infusion
- Serving with Herbaceous Sides

French Apple Cake with Caramel Glaze

- Decadence with Caramel
- Recipe: French Apple Cake with Caramel Glaze
- Caramel Drizzling Technique
- Dressing Up with Edible Flowers

Gluten-Free French Apple Cake

- Embracing Gluten-Free Baking
- Recipe: Gluten-Free French Apple Cake
- Flour Alternatives
- Nut Flour Options

Vegan French Apple Cake

- Plant-Based Baking Magic
- Recipe: Vegan French Apple Cake
- Egg and Dairy Substitutes
- Wholesome Vegan Frosting

French Apple Cake with Almonds

Cider-Infused French Apple Cake

Tips for Perfectly Caramelized Apples

Serving Suggestions and Pairings

Mastering French Apple Cake Baking Techniques

Chapter 1: Introduction to French Apple Cakes

The History of French Apple Cakes

French apple cakes, or "gâteaux aux pommes," hold a special place in the heart of French baking traditions. These delectable desserts have been enjoyed in France for centuries, with their roots tracing back to the lush orchards of Normandy and the charming patisseries of Paris. The history of French apple cakes is a journey through the country's culinary heritage.

Centuries ago, apples were cultivated in abundance throughout France, and the French quickly found creative ways to incorporate them into their cuisine. The first apple cake recipes emerged in rural regions where apples were plentiful, such as Normandy and Brittany. These early recipes were simple, rustic, and celebrated the natural sweetness of apples.

As time passed and culinary techniques evolved, French pastry chefs began to refine apple cake recipes, adding layers of complexity and sophistication. The resulting creations became a delightful balance of textures and flavors, showcasing the culinary mastery of French patisseries.

Regional Variations

One of the most intriguing aspects of French apple cakes is the wide array of regional variations. Each region in France has its unique twist on this classic dessert, making it a diverse and exciting culinary landscape to explore.

Normandy Apple Cake: Hailing from the Normandy region, this cake features thinly sliced apples and often includes a touch of Calvados, an apple brandy native to the area. It's a celebration of the region's rich apple orchards.

Tarte Tatin: Originating from the Hotel Tatin in Lamotte-Beuvron, this upside-down apple tart is known for its caramelized apples and buttery, flaky pastry. It's an iconic French dessert loved worldwide.

Breton Apple Cake (Far Breton aux Pommes): Brittany's version of apple cake is unique for its custardy texture. It's traditionally made with prunes, but apples are a delightful alternative.

Alsace-Style Apple Kugelhopf: The Alsace region brings its own flair with this apple cake that incorporates the flavors of the region, including almonds and raisins.

Savory Apple and Brie Tart: Some regions even put a savory twist on apple cakes, as seen in this tart featuring apples and creamy Brie cheese.

Why French Apple Cakes are Special

French apple cakes are celebrated not only for their regional diversity but also for their dedication to quality ingredients and precise techniques. What makes them truly special are:

Apples: France boasts an impressive variety of apple cultivars, each with its unique flavor profile. French apple cakes often feature apples like Golden Delicious, Granny Smith, or local varieties, which are carefully selected to complement the cake's overall taste.

Butter: French baking is renowned for its generous use of butter, which adds richness and a distinctive flavor to these cakes. The combination of butter and apples creates a delightful harmony.

Technique: French pastry chefs pay meticulous attention to technique, from slicing apples uniformly thin to achieving the perfect caramelization. These techniques elevate the final product.

Tradition: French apple cakes carry a deep sense of tradition. They are enjoyed during various occasions, from family gatherings to holiday celebrations, making them an integral part of French culture.

Ingredients Overview

While specific recipes may vary, the core ingredients in French apple cakes typically include:

- Fresh apples, peeled and thinly sliced

- All-purpose flour or a blend of flours for the batter
- Unsalted butter, often browned for a nutty flavor
- Eggs, which add structure and moisture
- Sugar, for sweetness and caramelization
- Baking powder or baking soda, for leavening
- A pinch of salt to enhance the flavors
- Flavor enhancers like vanilla extract, cinnamon, or spices

In the following chapters, we will delve into the world of French apple cakes, exploring both traditional and modern interpretations of these delightful desserts. Whether you're a seasoned baker or a novice in the kitchen, this cookbook will guide you through the art of creating these exquisite cakes, each with its unique charm.

Chapter 2: Essential Tools and Ingredients

In the world of French apple cakes, having the right tools and ingredients is the key to creating a masterpiece. This chapter will guide you through the essential kitchen equipment and ingredients you'll need to embark on your delicious baking journey.

Must-Have Kitchen Equipment

Before you begin baking, it's essential to equip your kitchen with the necessary tools to make the process smoother and more enjoyable. Here are some must-have kitchen items:

1. Mixing Bowls: Invest in a set of high-quality mixing bowls in various sizes. These are essential for combining ingredients, from batter to fillings.

2. Measuring Cups and Spoons: Precise measurements are crucial in baking. A set of measuring cups and spoons will help you achieve accurate results.

3. Whisk and Spatula: A whisk is ideal for blending wet ingredients, while a spatula ensures you can scrape every last bit of batter from your mixing bowl.

4. Stand Mixer or Hand Mixer: While not mandatory, a stand mixer or hand mixer makes mixing and beating easier, especially for recipes with a lot of batter.

5. Cake Pans and Tart Pans: Invest in round cake pans and tart pans with removable bottoms. These are perfect for creating beautiful and easy-to-release French apple cakes.

6. Parchment Paper: Line your pans with parchment paper to prevent sticking and make cake removal a breeze.

7. Peeler and Apple Corer: For prepping your apples, a good-quality peeler and corer will save you time and effort.

8. Zester and Grater: A zester or grater is handy for adding zest from citrus fruits, like lemons or oranges, to enhance the flavor of your cakes.

9. Pastry Brush: This is useful for applying glazes or butter to your cakes, giving them a beautiful finish.

10. Cooling Racks: Allow your cakes to cool properly by placing them on cooling racks. This prevents condensation from making them soggy.

Selecting the Perfect Apples

Apples are the star of the show in French apple cakes, so selecting the right ones is crucial. Here's what you should consider when choosing apples for your recipes:

1. Varieties: Different apple varieties offer various flavors and textures. Some popular choices for baking include Granny Smith (tart and firm), Honeycrisp (sweet and juicy), and Braeburn (sweet and slightly tart). Experiment to find your favorite.

2. Texture: Look for apples that are firm to the touch but not rock-hard. They should have a crisp texture that holds up during baking.

3. Taste: Consider the sweetness and tartness of the apples. Depending on your recipe, you may want a balance between sweet and tart flavors.

4. Freshness: Choose apples that are fresh, free from bruises or blemishes. Organic options can provide cleaner, pesticide-free choices.

Flour and Other Dry Ingredients

French apple cakes often require a blend of dry ingredients to create a perfect batter. Here's what you need to know:

1. Flour: All-purpose flour is the most versatile choice for most French apple cake recipes. However, you can experiment with whole wheat flour or almond flour for unique textures and flavors.

2. Sugar: Granulated sugar is commonly used, but brown sugar can add a delightful caramel note to your cakes. Powdered sugar is ideal for dusting the finished product.

3. Leavening Agents: Baking powder or baking soda is essential to help your cakes rise and become light and fluffy.

4. Salt: A pinch of salt enhances the overall flavor of your cakes, balancing sweetness and enhancing other ingredients' taste.

5. Spices: Common spices include ground cinnamon and nutmeg, which complement the apple's flavor beautifully.

Dairy and Non-Dairy Options

To accommodate different dietary preferences, consider these options for dairy and non-dairy ingredients:

1. Butter: Traditional French apple cakes use unsalted butter for richness. However, you can substitute with dairy-free alternatives like vegan butter or coconut oil for a dairy-free option.

2. Milk: Regular milk or non-dairy milk, such as almond, soy, or oat milk, can replace dairy milk in most recipes.

3. Eggs: Eggs provide structure and moisture. For vegan options, try using flax eggs (1 tablespoon ground flaxseed mixed with 3 tablespoons water per egg) or applesauce.

With these essential tools and ingredients in your kitchen arsenal, you're well-prepared to dive into the world of French apple cake baking. In the upcoming chapters, you'll put these items to good use as we explore a variety of French apple cake recipes, each with its own unique charm.

Chapter 3: Classic French Apple Cake

Recipe: Traditional French Apple Cake

The Classic French Apple Cake is a timeless masterpiece that embodies the essence of French baking. It's a cake that celebrates the natural sweetness of apples while showcasing the expertise of French pastry techniques.

Ingredients:

- 4 large apples, peeled, cored, and thinly sliced
- 1 cup all-purpose flour
- 1 teaspoon baking powder
- 1/4 teaspoon salt
- 1/2 cup unsalted butter, softened
- 1 cup granulated sugar
- 2 large eggs
- 1 teaspoon pure vanilla extract
- 2 tablespoons dark rum (optional)
- Powdered sugar, for dusting

Instructions:

Preheat your oven to 350°F (175°C). Grease and flour a 9-inch (23 cm) round cake pan or springform pan.

In a medium-sized bowl, whisk together the flour, baking powder, and salt. Set this dry mixture aside.

In a separate large bowl, cream the softened butter and granulated sugar together until light and fluffy, which takes about 2-3 minutes with an electric mixer.

Add the eggs, one at a time, beating well after each addition. Stir in the vanilla extract and dark rum (if using).

Gradually add the dry ingredients to the wet ingredients, mixing until just combined. Be careful not to overmix; it's okay if there are a few small lumps.

Gently fold in the thinly sliced apples, ensuring they are evenly distributed throughout the batter.

Pour the batter into the prepared pan, spreading it out evenly.

Bake for approximately 40-50 minutes or until the cake is golden brown and a toothpick inserted into the center comes out clean.

Remove the cake from the oven and let it cool in the pan for about 15 minutes. Then, transfer it to a wire rack to cool completely.

Once the cake has cooled, dust the top with powdered sugar for a delightful finish.

Tips for a Perfectly Moist Cake

Apple Selection: Choose apples with a balanced sweet-tart flavor, such as Granny Smith or Honeycrisp. Slicing them thinly ensures they soften and infuse the cake with their natural sweetness.

Avoid Overmixing: Overmixing the batter can lead to a dense cake. Mix until the dry ingredients are just incorporated to maintain a light and airy texture.

Dark Rum: The addition of dark rum is optional but adds a wonderful depth of flavor. If you prefer a non-alcoholic version, you can omit it or use apple juice as a substitute.

Cooling: Allow the cake to cool in the pan for a short while before transferring it to a wire rack. This helps prevent the cake from breaking apart.

Serving Suggestions

The Classic French Apple Cake is delightful on its own, but it can also be elevated with a few serving suggestions:

Whipped Cream: A dollop of freshly whipped cream adds a luxurious touch and contrasts beautifully with the cake's sweetness.

Caramel Sauce: Drizzle warm caramel sauce over individual slices for a decadent treat.

Vanilla Ice Cream: A scoop of quality vanilla ice cream is a classic pairing, creating a delightful mix of warm and cold.

Fresh Berries: Garnish with fresh berries like raspberries or blueberries for a burst of color and freshness.

This classic French apple cake is a testament to the elegance of French baking. Its simplicity highlights the natural flavors of apples while offering a satisfying, comforting dessert.

Chapter 4: Normandy Apple Cake

The Charm of Normandy

Nestled in the northwestern corner of France, Normandy is a region known for its picturesque landscapes, charming villages, and, of course, its apples. It's a place where apple orchards stretch as far as the eye can see, and apple-based delicacies hold a special place in the hearts of its residents.

Normandy's climate, with its mild temperatures and ample rainfall, creates the perfect conditions for apple cultivation. The region boasts numerous apple varieties, each with its unique flavor and texture. From crisp and tart apples like the Calville Blanc d'Hiver to the sweet and juicy Rouge Détour, Normandy's apples are a treasure trove for bakers.

Recipe: Normandy Apple Cake

The Normandy Apple Cake, or "Gâteau aux Pommes de Normandie," captures the essence of this charming region. It features thinly sliced apples that meld into the cake's tender crumb, creating a delightful contrast of textures.

Ingredients:

- 4 large apples (preferably a mix of sweet and tart varieties), peeled, cored, and thinly sliced
- 1 cup all-purpose flour
- 1 teaspoon baking powder
- A pinch of salt
- 1/2 cup unsalted butter, softened
- 1 cup granulated sugar
- 2 large eggs
- 1 teaspoon pure vanilla extract
- 2 tablespoons Calvados (apple brandy)
- Powdered sugar, for dusting

Instructions:

Preheat your oven to 350°F (175°C). Grease and flour a 9-inch (23 cm) round cake pan or springform pan.

In a medium-sized bowl, whisk together the flour, baking powder, and salt. Set this dry mixture aside.

In a separate large bowl, cream the softened butter and granulated sugar together until light and fluffy, which takes about 2-3 minutes with an electric mixer.

Add the eggs, one at a time, beating well after each addition. Stir in the vanilla extract and Calvados, which adds a delightful apple essence to the cake.

Gradually add the dry ingredients to the wet ingredients, mixing until just combined. Avoid overmixing to maintain a tender texture.

Gently fold in the thinly sliced apples, ensuring they are evenly distributed throughout the batter.

Pour the batter into the prepared pan, spreading it out evenly.

Bake for approximately 40-50 minutes or until the cake is golden brown and a toothpick inserted into the center comes out clean.

Remove the cake from the oven and let it cool in the pan for about 15 minutes. Then, transfer it to a wire rack to cool completely.

Once the cake has cooled, dust the top with powdered sugar for a touch of elegance.

A Taste of Calvados

Calvados, an apple brandy from Normandy, is a key ingredient that sets the Normandy Apple Cake apart. It adds a unique depth of flavor, enhancing the natural apple sweetness. If you don't have Calvados, you can substitute with another apple brandy or simply omit it for a non-alcoholic version. However, if you have the opportunity to use Calvados, it truly captures the spirit of Normandy.

Garnishing Ideas

The Normandy Apple Cake is a stunning dessert on its own, but you can take its presentation to the next level with these garnishing ideas:

Whipped Cream: A dollop of freshly whipped cream adds a creamy contrast to the cake's texture.

Caramel Drizzle: Drizzle warm caramel sauce over individual slices for an extra layer of sweetness.

Toasted Almonds: Sprinkle toasted sliced almonds on top for a delightful crunch.

Apple Slices: Thinly slice a few extra apples and arrange them decoratively on top of the cake for a beautiful finish.

The Normandy Apple Cake is a testament to the rich apple heritage of this charming French region. With its sweet and tart apple flavors and a touch of Calvados, it's a dessert that transports you to the orchards of Normandy with every bite.

Chapter 5: Tarte Tatin: A French Apple Upside-Down Cake

The Story Behind Tarte Tatin

Tarte Tatin, often referred to simply as "Tatin," is a beloved French pastry with a charming origin story. It was created at the Hôtel Tatin in Lamotte-Beuvron, a small town in the Loir-et-Cher region of central France.

The tale goes that the Tatin sisters, Stéphanie and Caroline, managed the hotel in the late 19th century. One day, as the story is told, Stéphanie accidentally overcooked her apple tart. In a hurry to salvage the dessert, she placed a layer of pastry over the caramelized apples, flipped it upside-down, and baked it again. When the tart emerged from the oven, it was a revelation—a beautifully caramelized, upside-down apple tart that became an instant sensation.

Today, Tarte Tatin is celebrated for its rich caramelized apples and flaky, buttery pastry. It's a dessert that captures the essence of rustic French cuisine and has become a symbol of French culinary excellence.

Recipe: Tarte Tatin

Tarte Tatin may seem intimidating, but with a little practice, you can master the art of caramelizing apples to perfection and create this exquisite dessert. Here's the recipe:

Ingredients:

- 6-8 medium-sized apples (preferably firm and slightly tart), peeled, cored, and halved
- 1 cup granulated sugar
- 1/2 cup unsalted butter
- 1 teaspoon pure vanilla extract
- 1 sheet of puff pastry, thawed
- A pinch of salt

Instructions:

Preheat your oven to 375°F (190°C).

In a 9-inch (23 cm) ovenproof skillet or Tatin dish, melt the butter over medium heat. Add the sugar and cook, stirring occasionally, until it caramelizes and turns a deep amber color. This should take about 10-12 minutes.

Remove the skillet from the heat and stir in the vanilla extract. Place the apple halves, rounded side down, in the caramel, packing them tightly. Return the skillet to low heat and cook for an additional 10 minutes, allowing the apples to absorb the caramel.

Roll out the puff pastry sheet to a size slightly larger than the skillet. Place the pastry over the apples, tucking the edges down the sides of the skillet.

Use a knife to make a few small cuts in the pastry to allow steam to escape.

Bake in the preheated oven for approximately 25-30 minutes, or until the pastry is golden brown and puffed.

Remove the skillet from the oven and let it cool for a few minutes. Be cautious as the caramel is extremely hot.

Place a serving platter over the skillet and, using oven mitts, carefully flip the Tarte Tatin onto the platter. The caramelized apples should now be on top, and the pastry on the bottom.

Allow the Tarte Tatin to cool slightly before serving.

Flipping Techniques

Flipping the Tarte Tatin is a crucial step in the process. Here are some tips to ensure a successful flip:

- Choose a skillet with a flat bottom and sturdy handles.
- Ensure the pastry is slightly larger than the skillet to cover the apples completely.
- Use oven mitts or a kitchen towel to protect your hands from the hot skillet.
- Place the serving platter upside down over the skillet, so the rim of the platter is against the rim of the skillet.
- Hold the skillet and platter firmly together and flip them quickly but smoothly. The caramelized apples should release easily onto the platter.

Pairing with Vanilla Ice Cream

Tarte Tatin is a delightful dessert on its own, but it reaches new heights when paired with creamy vanilla ice cream. The cool, creamy texture of the ice cream complements the warm, caramelized apples and flaky pastry perfectly. Serve a scoop of vanilla ice cream alongside each slice of Tarte Tatin for a decadent experience that balances sweet and cold with warm and rich.

Tarte Tatin is a celebration of French culinary innovation and the magic that can happen in the kitchen. It's a dessert that tells a story and captures the essence of French culture, making it a delightful addition to your French apple cake repertoire.

Chapter 6: Breton Apple Cake: Far Breton aux Pommes

Breton Culinary Traditions

Breton cuisine is known for its hearty and rustic flavors, influenced by the region's coastal location and agricultural heritage. Brittany, located in the northwest of France, is famous for its seafood, dairy products, and delicious pastries. Among the region's culinary treasures is the Breton Apple Cake, known as "Far Breton aux Pommes."

Breton cuisine often celebrates simplicity and local ingredients, and this apple cake is no exception. It combines the goodness of fresh apples with a custardy batter, creating a dessert that's comforting and deeply satisfying.

Recipe: Far Breton aux Pommes

The Far Breton aux Pommes is a delightful variation of the classic Far Breton, with the addition of apples providing a sweet and tart contrast to the custard-like texture of the cake.

Ingredients:

- 3-4 apples (preferably tart), peeled, cored, and thinly sliced
- 1 cup all-purpose flour
- 1/2 cup granulated sugar
- A pinch of salt
- 3 large eggs
- 2 cups whole milk
- 1 teaspoon pure vanilla extract
- 2 tablespoons whiskey or dark rum (optional)
- Butter, for greasing the baking dish
- Powdered sugar, for dusting (optional)

Instructions:

Preheat your oven to 350°F (175°C). Grease a 9-inch (23 cm) round baking dish or tart pan with butter.

In a large mixing bowl, whisk together the flour, granulated sugar, and a pinch of salt.

In another bowl, beat the eggs, and then gradually add the milk and vanilla extract, whisking until well combined.

Pour the wet ingredients into the dry ingredients and whisk until you have a smooth batter.

Stir in the whiskey or dark rum (if using). This addition adds depth and flavor to the cake but is entirely optional.

Arrange the thinly sliced apples evenly in the greased baking dish.

Pour the batter over the apples, ensuring they are well coated.

Bake in the preheated oven for about 40-50 minutes, or until the top is golden brown and the center is set. The cake should have a custardy texture.

Remove the cake from the oven and let it cool for a few minutes.

Optionally, dust the top with powdered sugar for a touch of sweetness and an elegant finish.

Unique Texture of Far

What sets Far Breton aux Pommes apart is its distinctive texture. The combination of a custardy batter and the natural moisture from the apples creates a dessert that's velvety and moist, almost like a clafoutis. It's comforting, satisfying, and perfect for enjoying with a cup of coffee or tea.

Whiskey or Rum Additions

The addition of whiskey or dark rum to this recipe is a nod to Breton's maritime heritage and the influence of the sea on its cuisine. These spirits add warmth and depth to the cake's flavor, making it even more enticing. However, if you prefer a non-alcoholic version, you can omit them without compromising the overall deliciousness of the cake.

The Far Breton aux Pommes is a wonderful testament to the rustic and comforting flavors of Brittany. It's a dessert that embodies the region's culinary traditions and provides a delightful twist on the classic Far Breton.

Chapter 7: Apple and Calvados Cake

A Toast to Calvados

Calvados, an apple brandy hailing from the Normandy region of France, is a spirit rich in tradition and flavor. Named after the department in which it's produced, Calvados is crafted from carefully selected apples and then aged in oak barrels, resulting in a spirit that's aromatic, complex, and truly unique.

The marriage of apples and Calvados is a match made in culinary heaven. Calvados adds a layer of depth and complexity to the sweet, fruity flavor of apples, creating a delightful fusion of taste and aroma.

Recipe: Apple and Calvados Cake

The Apple and Calvados Cake is a masterpiece that highlights the exquisite combination of apples and Calvados in a cake that's both rich in flavor and moist in texture. Here's the recipe:

Ingredients:

For the Cake:

- 3-4 medium-sized apples (a mix of sweet and tart varieties), peeled, cored, and diced
- 1 tablespoon lemon juice (to prevent apple browning)
- 1 1/2 cups all-purpose flour
- 2 teaspoons baking powder
- 1/2 teaspoon salt
- 1/2 cup unsalted butter, softened
- 1 cup granulated sugar
- 2 large eggs
- 1 teaspoon pure vanilla extract
- 1/4 cup Calvados (apple brandy)

For the Aromatic Calvados Glaze:

- 1/4 cup unsalted butter
- 1/4 cup granulated sugar
- 1/4 cup Calvados (apple brandy)

Instructions:
For the Cake:
Preheat your oven to 350°F (175°C). Grease and flour a 9-inch (23 cm) round cake pan.

In a bowl, toss the diced apples with lemon juice to prevent browning. Set them aside.

In a separate bowl, whisk together the flour, baking powder, and salt. Set this dry mixture aside.

In a large bowl, cream the softened butter and granulated sugar together until light and fluffy, which takes about 2-3 minutes with an electric mixer.

Add the eggs, one at a time, beating well after each addition. Stir in the vanilla extract.

Gradually add the dry ingredients to the wet ingredients, mixing until just combined.

Gently fold in the diced apples, ensuring they are evenly distributed throughout the batter.

Pour the batter into the prepared pan, spreading it out evenly.

Bake for approximately 40-50 minutes or until the cake is golden brown and a toothpick inserted into the center comes out clean.

While the cake is baking, prepare the Aromatic Calvados Glaze.

For the Aromatic Calvados Glaze:
In a small saucepan over low heat, melt the butter and granulated sugar, stirring until the sugar is dissolved.

Remove the saucepan from the heat and stir in the Calvados.

Assembly:
Once the cake has finished baking, remove it from the oven and let it cool in the pan for about 10 minutes.

While the cake is still warm, use a skewer or fork to poke several holes all over the top of the cake.

Drizzle the Aromatic Calvados Glaze evenly over the warm cake, allowing it to seep into the holes and infuse the cake with Calvados flavor.

Serving in Style

The Apple and Calvados Cake is a work of art that deserves to be served with style. Here are some serving suggestions to make your dessert truly exceptional:

Dust with Powdered Sugar: Before serving, dust the top of the cake with powdered sugar for an elegant finish.

Whipped Cream: Serve each slice with a dollop of freshly whipped cream to add a creamy contrast to the cake's flavor and texture.

Calvados Pairing: To complement the Calvados-infused cake, consider serving small glasses of Calvados alongside the dessert, allowing guests to savor the full experience of this delightful spirit.

The Apple and Calvados Cake is a celebration of the rich flavors of Normandy and the exquisite pairing of apples and Calvados. It's a dessert that captures the essence of French culinary craftsmanship and offers a memorable indulgence for those who appreciate the finer things in life.

Chapter 8: Rustic French Apple Galette

Rustic Elegance in a Galette

The French Apple Galette embodies the perfect balance between rustic charm and sophisticated flavors. Galettes are renowned for their simplicity, with a free-form, hand-folded pastry that celebrates the natural beauty of fresh ingredients.

The beauty of a galette lies in its imperfections. Unlike a traditional pie or tart, a galette doesn't demand a perfectly rolled-out crust or precisely arranged filling. Instead, it welcomes a relaxed and rustic approach, where the pastry is folded gently over the fruit, creating an elegantly uneven, golden crust.

Recipe: Rustic French Apple Galette

The Rustic French Apple Galette is a delightful dessert that captures the essence of French baking. It's perfect for those who appreciate the combination of tender, spiced apples and a flaky, buttery pastry. Here's the recipe:

Ingredients:

For the Pastry:

- 1 1/4 cups all-purpose flour
- 1/2 teaspoon salt
- 1/2 cup unsalted butter, cold and diced
- 1/4 cup ice water (approximately)

For the Filling:

- 3-4 medium-sized apples (a mix of sweet and tart varieties), peeled, cored, and thinly sliced
- 1/4 cup granulated sugar
- 1 teaspoon ground cinnamon
- A pinch of nutmeg (optional)

- 1 tablespoon lemon juice
- 2 tablespoons unsalted butter, diced

For Finishing:

- 1 egg, beaten (for egg wash)
- 1 tablespoon granulated sugar (for sprinkling)

Instructions:

For the Pastry:

In a food processor, combine the flour and salt. Add the cold, diced butter and pulse until the mixture resembles coarse crumbs.

Gradually add the ice water while pulsing, just until the dough begins to come together. Be cautious not to overmix.

Turn the dough out onto a lightly floured surface and gently knead it into a disk. Wrap it in plastic wrap and refrigerate for at least 30 minutes.

For the Filling:

In a bowl, toss the thinly sliced apples with granulated sugar, ground cinnamon, and a pinch of nutmeg (if using). Add lemon juice to prevent browning.

Assembly:

Preheat your oven to 375°F (190°C).

On a floured surface, roll out the chilled pastry dough into a rough circle, about 12 inches (30 cm) in diameter. It doesn't need to be perfectly round.

Carefully transfer the rolled-out pastry to a parchment paper-lined baking sheet.

Arrange the seasoned apple slices in the center of the pastry, leaving a border of about 2 inches (5 cm) around the edges.

Fold the edges of the pastry over the apples, pleating as you go. This creates the rustic, free-form shape of the galette.

Dot the diced butter over the apples.

Brush the edges of the pastry with the beaten egg and sprinkle with granulated sugar.

Bake in the preheated oven for approximately 35-40 minutes, or until the pastry is golden brown and the apples are tender.

Perfect Galette Presentation

A Rustic French Apple Galette deserves to be presented with care and attention to detail. Here are some tips for achieving the perfect galette presentation:

Parchment Paper: Line your baking sheet with parchment paper to prevent sticking and make it easier to transfer the galette.

Egg Wash: Brushing the pastry edges with an egg wash before baking gives them a beautiful golden shine.

Sugar Sprinkle: Sprinkling granulated sugar over the egg-washed edges not only adds a touch of sweetness but also creates a lovely, slightly crunchy texture.

Rustic Folds: Embrace the rustic nature of the galette by not striving for perfect folds. Let the pastry fold naturally, creating a charming, handcrafted look.

Serve Warm: A Rustic French Apple Galette is best served warm, with a scoop of vanilla ice cream or a dollop of whipped cream.

The Rustic French Apple Galette embodies the simplicity and elegance of French baking. Its free-form pastry and spiced apple filling make it a delightful dessert for any occasion, whether enjoyed as a casual treat or a refined finish to a special meal.

Chapter 9: Apple and Cinnamon Clafoutis

Clafoutis: Beyond Cherries

Clafoutis is a classic French dessert that originated in the Limousin region of France. Traditionally, it's made with sweet cherries, but it's a versatile dessert that can showcase a variety of fruits, including apples. The essence of clafoutis lies in its custardy batter, which encases tender, baked fruit in a delicious embrace.

Clafoutis is often enjoyed as a comforting dessert or even as a delightful breakfast treat. Its simplicity, elegance, and warm, custardy texture make it a favorite in French homes and restaurants alike.

Recipe: Apple and Cinnamon Clafoutis

The Apple and Cinnamon Clafoutis is a delightful twist on the traditional recipe. The combination of apples and cinnamon creates a comforting, aromatic dessert that's perfect for any season. Here's the recipe:

Ingredients:

- 3-4 medium-sized apples (a mix of sweet and tart varieties), peeled, cored, and thinly sliced
- 1/2 cup all-purpose flour
- 1/2 cup granulated sugar
- 1/4 teaspoon salt
- 1 teaspoon ground cinnamon
- 3 large eggs
- 1 cup whole milk
- 1 teaspoon pure vanilla extract
- Butter, for greasing the baking dish
- Powdered sugar, for dusting

Instructions:

Preheat your oven to 350°F (175°C). Grease a 9-inch (23 cm) round baking dish or pie pan with butter.

In a large mixing bowl, whisk together the flour, granulated sugar, salt, and ground cinnamon.

In a separate bowl, beat the eggs, and then add the whole milk and vanilla extract. Whisk until well combined.

Gradually add the wet ingredients to the dry ingredients, whisking until you have a smooth batter.

Arrange the thinly sliced apples evenly in the greased baking dish.

Pour the batter over the apples, ensuring they are well coated.

Bake in the preheated oven for approximately 35-45 minutes or until the clafoutis is set and has a golden brown top.

Remove the clafoutis from the oven and let it cool for a few minutes.

Optionally, dust the top with powdered sugar for a touch of sweetness and an elegant finish.

Spice Variations

While this recipe features ground cinnamon, you can experiment with different spices to create unique variations of Apple and Cinnamon Clafoutis:

Nutmeg: Add a pinch of ground nutmeg for a warm, nutty flavor that complements the apples beautifully.

Cardamom: Replace or combine with cinnamon for a hint of exotic spice.

Allspice: The warmth of allspice pairs wonderfully with apples and adds complexity to the clafoutis.

Ginger: Freshly grated ginger or ground ginger can lend a zesty, slightly spicy kick to the dessert.

A Dusting of Powdered Sugar

Dusting the top of the clafoutis with powdered sugar is not only for visual appeal but also for a delightful hint of sweetness. You can use a fine-mesh sieve to achieve an even, delicate layer of powdered sugar. This simple touch elevates the dessert's presentation and enhances its flavor.

The Apple and Cinnamon Clafoutis is a comforting dessert that embodies the warmth and charm of French baking. Its custardy texture and aromatic spices make it a delightful treat to enjoy with a cup of tea or as a finishing touch to a cozy meal.

Chapter 10: Alsace-Style Apple Kugelhopf

The Alsace Region's Influence

Alsace, a region in northeastern France known for its stunning landscapes, charming villages, and unique blend of French and German cultures, is also celebrated for its rich culinary traditions. One of the standout desserts from this region is the Alsace-Style Apple Kugelhopf.

Kugelhopf, a classic Alsatian pastry, is characterized by its distinctive shape—a fluted, ring-shaped cake. It's a dessert that showcases the region's love for apples, a staple in Alsace's orchards. This dessert combines the comforting flavors of apples with the elegance of almond filling and a crown of slivered almonds.

Recipe: Alsace-Style Apple Kugelhopf

The Alsace-Style Apple Kugelhopf is a delightful treat that brings together the essence of Alsace in every bite. Here's the recipe:

Ingredients:

For the Kugelhopf:

- 3-4 medium-sized apples (a mix of sweet and tart varieties), peeled, cored, and thinly sliced
- 1 tablespoon lemon juice (to prevent apple browning)
- 2 1/4 cups all-purpose flour
- 2 1/4 teaspoons active dry yeast
- 1/2 cup warm milk (about 110°F or 43°C)
- 1/4 cup granulated sugar
- 1/2 teaspoon salt
- 3 large eggs
- 1/2 cup unsalted butter, softened

For the Rich Almond Filling:

- 1 cup ground almonds
- 1/2 cup granulated sugar
- 2 large egg whites
- 1 teaspoon almond extract

For the Crown of Slivered Almonds:

- 1/4 cup slivered almonds

For Glazing (Optional):

- 1/4 cup apricot jam, warmed

Instructions:

For the Kugelhopf:

In a bowl, toss the thinly sliced apples with lemon juice to prevent browning. Set them aside.

In a small bowl, dissolve the active dry yeast in the warm milk and let it sit for about 5 minutes, or until frothy.

In a large mixing bowl, combine the flour, granulated sugar, and salt.

Add the yeast mixture and mix until a dough forms.

Add the eggs one at a time, mixing well after each addition.

Gradually add the softened butter and knead the dough until it's smooth and elastic. This can take about 10-15 minutes.

Gently fold in the thinly sliced apples until they are evenly distributed throughout the dough.

For the Rich Almond Filling:

In a separate bowl, combine the ground almonds, granulated sugar, egg whites, and almond extract. Mix until you have a smooth almond filling.

Assembly:

Grease a kugelhopf or Bundt cake pan generously with butter.

Sprinkle the slivered almonds evenly over the bottom of the pan.

Carefully place spoonfuls of the rich almond filling on top of the slivered almonds.

Add the apple dough on top of the almond filling, spreading it out evenly.

Cover the pan with a clean kitchen towel and let it rise in a warm place for about 1 hour, or until it has doubled in size.

Preheat your oven to 350°F (175°C).

Bake the kugelhopf in the preheated oven for approximately 35-45 minutes, or until it's golden brown and a toothpick inserted into the center comes out clean.

For Glazing (Optional):

Warm the apricot jam in a small saucepan over low heat until it's liquid.

Brush the warm apricot jam over the top of the kugelhopf for a shiny glaze.

The Alsace-Style Apple Kugelhopf is a masterpiece that captures the essence of Alsace's culinary heritage. Its fluted shape, rich almond filling, and crown of slivered almonds create a stunning dessert that's both visually appealing and a delight for the taste buds.

Chapter 11: Savory Apple and Brie Tart

Savory Side of French Apple Cakes

While sweet apple cakes often take the spotlight, it's important not to overlook the savory possibilities of apples in French cuisine. The Savory Apple and Brie Tart is a testament to this delightful alternative, combining the sweetness of apples with the creamy richness of Brie cheese in a flaky, savory pastry.

This tart celebrates the versatility of apples, showcasing how they can transition effortlessly from sweet desserts to savory delights. It's a wonderful addition to your repertoire of French apple-inspired recipes.

Recipe: Savory Apple and Brie Tart

The Savory Apple and Brie Tart is a flavorful treat that balances the sweetness of apples with the creamy, slightly tangy notes of Brie cheese. Here's the recipe:

Ingredients:

For the Pastry:

- 1 1/4 cups all-purpose flour
- 1/2 teaspoon salt
- 1/2 cup unsalted butter, cold and diced
- 1/4 cup ice water (approximately)

For the Filling:

- 2-3 medium-sized apples (a mix of sweet and tart varieties), peeled, cored, and thinly sliced
- 6 ounces (about 170 grams) Brie cheese, rind removed, and cut into small pieces
- 1/4 cup caramelized onions (optional, for added depth of flavor)
- 1 tablespoon olive oil

- 1 teaspoon fresh thyme leaves (or 1/2 teaspoon dried thyme)
- Salt and freshly ground black pepper, to taste

For Garnish:

- Fresh thyme sprigs or chopped fresh herbs (such as parsley or chives)

Instructions:
For the Pastry:
In a food processor, combine the flour and salt. Add the cold, diced butter and pulse until the mixture resembles coarse crumbs.

Gradually add the ice water while pulsing, just until the dough begins to come together. Be cautious not to overmix.

Turn the dough out onto a lightly floured surface and gently knead it into a disk. Wrap it in plastic wrap and refrigerate for at least 30 minutes.

For the Filling:
In a large skillet, heat the olive oil over medium heat. Add the thinly sliced apples and cook for about 3-5 minutes, or until they begin to soften. Remove them from the skillet and set them aside.

In the same skillet, add the caramelized onions (if using) and sauté for a couple of minutes until heated through.

Assembly:
Preheat your oven to 375°F (190°C).

On a floured surface, roll out the chilled pastry dough into a circle, about 12 inches (30 cm) in diameter.

Carefully transfer the rolled-out pastry to a parchment paper-lined baking sheet or tart pan.

Arrange the cooked apples and caramelized onions evenly over the pastry, leaving a border of about 1 inch (2.5 cm) around the edges.

Scatter the pieces of Brie cheese over the apples and onions.

Sprinkle fresh thyme leaves (or dried thyme) over the filling.

Season with salt and freshly ground black pepper to taste.

Carefully fold the edges of the pastry over the filling, creating a rustic, free-form tart.

Bake in the preheated oven for approximately 25-30 minutes, or until the pastry is golden brown and the cheese is melted and bubbly.

For Garnish:

Once the tart is out of the oven, garnish it with fresh thyme sprigs or chopped fresh herbs.

The Savory Apple and Brie Tart is a testament to the versatility of apples in French cuisine. Its combination of sweet apples, creamy Brie cheese, and aromatic thyme creates a harmonious and delightful savory dish. It can be served as an appetizer, a side dish, or even a light lunch, making it a versatile addition to your recipe collection.

Chapter 12: Provencal Olive Oil Apple Cake

Mediterranean Flavors in a Cake

Provence, a region in southeastern France blessed with abundant sunshine and a Mediterranean climate, is celebrated for its rich culinary traditions. The Provencal Olive Oil Apple Cake brings the essence of this beautiful region to your dessert table, infusing the sweet, comforting flavors of apples with the richness of olive oil.

This cake embodies the Mediterranean spirit, balancing the fruity sweetness of apples with the robust, slightly peppery notes of high-quality olive oil. It's a delightful fusion of sweet and savory that pays homage to the sunny flavors of Provence.

Recipe: Provencal Olive Oil Apple Cake

The Provencal Olive Oil Apple Cake is a unique and flavorful dessert that showcases the versatility of olive oil in baking. Here's the recipe:

Ingredients:

For the Cake:

- 3-4 medium-sized apples (a mix of sweet and tart varieties), peeled, cored, and thinly sliced
- 1 tablespoon lemon juice (to prevent apple browning)
- 1 1/2 cups all-purpose flour
- 1 1/2 teaspoons baking powder
- 1/2 teaspoon salt
- 3/4 cup granulated sugar
- 2 large eggs
- 1/2 cup high-quality extra virgin olive oil
- 1/2 cup whole milk
- 1 teaspoon pure vanilla extract

For the Olive Oil Infusion:

- 1/4 cup high-quality extra virgin olive oil
- Zest of 1 lemon
- 1 teaspoon dried lavender buds (optional, for a Provencal touch)

For Serving with Herbaceous Sides:

- Fresh thyme sprigs or rosemary sprigs
- A drizzle of high-quality extra virgin olive oil
- A sprinkle of flaky sea salt

Instructions:
For the Cake:
Preheat your oven to 350°F (175°C). Grease and flour a 9-inch (23 cm) round cake pan.

In a bowl, toss the thinly sliced apples with lemon juice to prevent browning. Set them aside.

In a separate bowl, whisk together the flour, baking powder, and salt.

In a large mixing bowl, beat the granulated sugar and eggs together until light and fluffy, which takes about 2-3 minutes with an electric mixer.

Gradually add the olive oil, continuing to mix until well combined.

Add the whole milk and pure vanilla extract, continuing to mix until you have a smooth batter.

Gradually add the dry ingredients to the wet ingredients, mixing until just combined.

Gently fold in the thinly sliced apples, ensuring they are evenly distributed throughout the batter.

For the Olive Oil Infusion:
In a small saucepan, heat the olive oil, lemon zest, and dried lavender buds (if using) over low heat until the oil is warm. Remove from heat and let it steep for about 10 minutes. Strain out the lemon zest and lavender buds, leaving you with fragrant, lemon-infused olive oil.

Assembly:

Pour the prepared cake batter into the greased and floured cake pan.

Drizzle the olive oil infusion evenly over the top of the batter.

Bake in the preheated oven for approximately 30-35 minutes, or until the cake is golden brown and a toothpick inserted into the center comes out clean.

For Serving with Herbaceous Sides:

Once the cake is out of the oven, garnish it with fresh thyme sprigs or rosemary sprigs for a herbaceous touch.

Drizzle a bit more high-quality extra virgin olive oil over the cake, and sprinkle a pinch of flaky sea salt for a burst of Mediterranean flavor.

The Provencal Olive Oil Apple Cake is a celebration of Mediterranean flavors, blending the warmth of olive oil, the brightness of lemon, and the sweetness of apples. It's a dessert that invites you to savor the simple pleasures of Provence and the art of olive oil-infused baking.

Chapter 13: French Apple Cake with Caramel Glaze

Decadence with Caramel

Indulgence meets tradition in the French Apple Cake with Caramel Glaze. Caramel, with its rich, buttery sweetness, takes the classic French apple cake to new heights of decadence. This dessert is a celebration of contrasts—tender apples meet velvety caramel in a cake that's both rustic and refined.

The caramel glaze drizzled generously over the cake adds a layer of depth and richness that elevates this dessert to a level of pure decadence. Each bite is a harmonious blend of sweet and slightly salty, a testament to the artistry of French baking.

Recipe: French Apple Cake with Caramel Glaze

The French Apple Cake with Caramel Glaze is a sumptuous treat that combines the comforting flavors of apples with the luxurious touch of caramel. Here's the recipe:

Ingredients:

For the Cake:

- 3-4 medium-sized apples (a mix of sweet and tart varieties), peeled, cored, and diced
- 1 tablespoon lemon juice (to prevent apple browning)
- 1 1/2 cups all-purpose flour
- 1 1/2 teaspoons baking powder
- 1/2 teaspoon salt
- 1/2 cup unsalted butter, softened
- 1 cup granulated sugar
- 2 large eggs
- 1 teaspoon pure vanilla extract
- 1/4 cup whole milk

For the Caramel Glaze:

- 1/2 cup granulated sugar
- 1/4 cup unsalted butter
- 1/4 cup heavy cream
- A pinch of salt

For Dressing Up with Edible Flowers:

- Fresh edible flowers, such as violets or pansies (for garnish)

Instructions:
For the Cake:
Preheat your oven to 350°F (175°C). Grease and flour a 9-inch (23 cm) round cake pan.

In a bowl, toss the diced apples with lemon juice to prevent browning. Set them aside.

In a separate bowl, whisk together the flour, baking powder, and salt.

In a large mixing bowl, cream the softened butter and granulated sugar together until light and fluffy, which takes about 2-3 minutes with an electric mixer.

Add the eggs, one at a time, beating well after each addition. Stir in the pure vanilla extract.

Gradually add the dry ingredients to the wet ingredients, mixing until just combined.

Stir in the whole milk until you have a smooth batter.

Gently fold in the diced apples, ensuring they are evenly distributed throughout the batter.

For the Caramel Glaze:
In a small saucepan over medium-low heat, melt the granulated sugar, stirring constantly until it turns a rich amber color.

Remove the saucepan from the heat and add the unsalted butter, heavy cream, and a pinch of salt. Be cautious, as the mixture may bubble up.

Return the saucepan to low heat and continue stirring until the caramel is smooth and well combined. Remove from heat and let it cool slightly.

Assembly:

Pour the prepared cake batter into the greased and floured cake pan.

Bake in the preheated oven for approximately 30-35 minutes, or until the cake is golden brown and a toothpick inserted into the center comes out clean.

For Dressing Up with Edible Flowers:

Once the cake is out of the oven and slightly cooled, drizzle the warm caramel glaze generously over the top.

Garnish the cake with fresh edible flowers, such as violets or pansies, for a touch of elegance and a pop of color.

The French Apple Cake with Caramel Glaze is a luxurious treat that combines the sweetness of apples with the opulence of caramel. It's a dessert that showcases the art of French baking, where simplicity meets indulgence in a symphony of flavor and texture.

Chapter 14: Gluten-Free French Apple Cake

Embracing Gluten-Free Baking

For those with dietary restrictions or sensitivities, embracing gluten-free baking opens up a world of possibilities while ensuring that everyone can enjoy the comforting flavors of French apple cake. The Gluten-Free French Apple Cake is a testament to the creativity and adaptability of gluten-free baking, allowing you to savor the classic dessert without compromising on taste or texture.

In this chapter, we'll explore how to make a delicious Gluten-Free French Apple Cake using alternative flours and nut flour options. Whether you follow a gluten-free diet by choice or necessity, this recipe ensures that you can still indulge in the joy of French apple cake.

Recipe: Gluten-Free French Apple Cake

The Gluten-Free French Apple Cake is a delightful treat that captures the essence of the classic dessert while catering to gluten-free needs. Here's the recipe:

Ingredients:

For the Cake:

- 3-4 medium-sized apples (a mix of sweet and tart varieties), peeled, cored, and diced
- 1 tablespoon lemon juice (to prevent apple browning)
- 1 1/4 cups gluten-free flour blend (look for a blend that includes xanthan gum)
- 1 1/2 teaspoons gluten-free baking powder
- 1/2 teaspoon salt
- 1/2 cup unsalted butter, softened
- 1 cup granulated sugar
- 2 large eggs
- 1 teaspoon pure vanilla extract

- 1/4 cup whole milk

For Nut Flour Options:

- Replace 1/4 cup of the gluten-free flour blend with almond flour, hazelnut flour, or chestnut flour for added richness and flavor.

Instructions:
For the Cake:
Preheat your oven to 350°F (175°C). Grease and flour a 9-inch (23 cm) round cake pan with gluten-free flour.

In a bowl, toss the diced apples with lemon juice to prevent browning. Set them aside.

In a separate bowl, whisk together the gluten-free flour blend, gluten-free baking powder, and salt.

In a large mixing bowl, cream the softened butter and granulated sugar together until light and fluffy, which takes about 2-3 minutes with an electric mixer.

Add the eggs, one at a time, beating well after each addition. Stir in the pure vanilla extract.

Gradually add the dry ingredients to the wet ingredients, mixing until just combined.

Stir in the whole milk until you have a smooth batter.

Gently fold in the diced apples, ensuring they are evenly distributed throughout the batter.

For Nut Flour Options:
If you choose to use nut flour, replace 1/4 cup of the gluten-free flour blend with your selected nut flour. This adds a unique richness and depth of flavor to the cake.

Assembly:
Pour the prepared cake batter into the greased and floured cake pan.

Bake in the preheated oven for approximately 30-35 minutes, or until the cake is golden brown and a toothpick inserted into the center comes out clean.

The Gluten-Free French Apple Cake is a testament to the adaptability of baking without gluten. With the right flour blend and optional nut flour additions, you can enjoy a delicious, gluten-free version of this classic French dessert. It's proof that flavor and texture can thrive in the absence of gluten.

Chapter 15: Vegan French Apple Cake

Plant-Based Baking Magic

Vegan baking is a realm of culinary creativity that celebrates the magic of plant-based ingredients. The Vegan French Apple Cake is a testament to the versatility of vegan baking, where traditional ingredients like eggs and dairy are replaced with wholesome plant-based alternatives, resulting in a delightful dessert that's entirely vegan-friendly.

This chapter explores how to make a delicious Vegan French Apple Cake, with a focus on egg and dairy substitutes that bring the classic dessert to life without compromising on flavor or texture. Whether you follow a vegan lifestyle or simply wish to enjoy a plant-based dessert, this recipe offers a delicious solution.

Recipe: Vegan French Apple Cake

The Vegan French Apple Cake is a delightful plant-based treat that captures the essence of the classic dessert. Here's the recipe:

Ingredients:

For the Cake:

- 3-4 medium-sized apples (a mix of sweet and tart varieties), peeled, cored, and diced
- 1 tablespoon lemon juice (to prevent apple browning)
- 1 1/4 cups all-purpose flour (or a gluten-free flour blend for a gluten-free option)
- 1 1/2 teaspoons baking powder
- 1/2 teaspoon salt
- 1/2 cup plant-based butter, softened (such as vegan margarine)
- 1 cup granulated sugar
- 1/4 cup unsweetened applesauce (as an egg substitute)
- 1 teaspoon pure vanilla extract
- 1/4 cup plant-based milk (such as almond, soy, or oat milk)

For Wholesome Vegan Frosting:

- 1/4 cup powdered sugar (ensure it's vegan)
- 1-2 tablespoons plant-based milk (adjust for desired consistency)
- A pinch of ground cinnamon (optional, for added flavor)

Instructions:

For the Cake:

Preheat your oven to 350°F (175°C). Grease and flour a 9-inch (23 cm) round cake pan.

In a bowl, toss the diced apples with lemon juice to prevent browning. Set them aside.

In a separate bowl, whisk together the all-purpose flour (or gluten-free flour blend), baking powder, and salt.

In a large mixing bowl, cream the softened plant-based butter and granulated sugar together until light and fluffy, which takes about 2-3 minutes with an electric mixer.

Add the unsweetened applesauce (as an egg substitute) and pure vanilla extract, continuing to mix until well combined.

Gradually add the dry ingredients to the wet ingredients, mixing until just combined.

Stir in the plant-based milk until you have a smooth batter.

Gently fold in the diced apples, ensuring they are evenly distributed throughout the batter.

For Wholesome Vegan Frosting:

In a small bowl, whisk together the powdered sugar, plant-based milk, and a pinch of ground cinnamon (if using) until you have a smooth, pourable frosting. Adjust the milk quantity for your desired consistency.

Assembly:

Pour the prepared cake batter into the greased and floured cake pan.

Bake in the preheated oven for approximately 30-35 minutes, or until the cake is golden brown and a toothpick inserted into the center comes out clean.

Once the cake has cooled slightly, drizzle the wholesome vegan frosting over the top for added sweetness and flavor.

The Vegan French Apple Cake is a delicious plant-based dessert that embraces the magic of vegan baking. With egg and dairy substitutes, you can enjoy the flavors and textures of the classic French apple cake while staying true to your vegan lifestyle or dietary preferences.

Chapter 16: French Apple Cake with Almonds

The Crunch of Almonds

Almonds bring a delightful crunch and a nutty richness to the classic French apple cake, transforming it into a delightful variation that appeals to almond lovers. The French Apple Cake with Almonds is a celebration of texture and flavor, where the tender sweetness of apples meets the earthy, nutty notes of toasted almonds.

This chapter explores how to make a delicious French Apple Cake with Almonds, including a toasted almond topping that adds an extra layer of indulgence. Whether you're an almond enthusiast or simply curious about this delightful combination, this recipe will satisfy your cravings for a textural delight.

Recipe: French Apple Cake with Almonds

The French Apple Cake with Almonds is a delightful twist on the classic dessert, showcasing the wonderful crunch and flavor of toasted almonds. Here's the recipe:

Ingredients:

For the Cake:

- 3-4 medium-sized apples (a mix of sweet and tart varieties), peeled, cored, and thinly sliced
- 1 tablespoon lemon juice (to prevent apple browning)
- 1 1/2 cups all-purpose flour
- 1 1/2 teaspoons baking powder
- 1/2 teaspoon salt
- 1/2 cup unsalted butter, softened
- 1 cup granulated sugar
- 2 large eggs
- 1 teaspoon pure vanilla extract
- 1/4 cup whole milk

For the Toasted Almond Topping:

- 1/2 cup sliced almonds, toasted

For Almond Lovers' Tips:

- Additional ways to incorporate almonds into your French apple cake for maximum flavor and crunch.

Instructions:

For the Cake:

Preheat your oven to 350°F (175°C). Grease and flour a 9-inch (23 cm) round cake pan.

In a bowl, toss the thinly sliced apples with lemon juice to prevent browning. Set them aside.

In a separate bowl, whisk together the flour, baking powder, and salt.

In a large mixing bowl, cream the softened butter and granulated sugar together until light and fluffy, which takes about 2-3 minutes with an electric mixer.

Add the eggs, one at a time, beating well after each addition. Stir in the pure vanilla extract.

Gradually add the dry ingredients to the wet ingredients, mixing until just combined.

Stir in the whole milk until you have a smooth batter.

Gently fold in the thinly sliced apples, ensuring they are evenly distributed throughout the batter.

For the Toasted Almond Topping:

In a dry skillet over medium-low heat, toast the sliced almonds until they turn golden brown and become fragrant. Be attentive, as they can burn quickly. Remove from heat and let them cool.

For Almond Lovers' Tips:

Explore additional ways to incorporate almonds into your French apple cake, such as incorporating almond flour into the batter or adding a drizzle of almond extract for an extra burst of almond flavor.

Consider using almond butter or almond cream as a filling between layers for a truly indulgent almond experience.

The French Apple Cake with Almonds is a delightful combination of sweet, tender apples and the satisfying crunch of toasted almonds. This variation adds a layer of texture and flavor that's sure to please almond enthusiasts and dessert lovers alike.

Chapter 17: Cider-Infused French Apple Cake

Apple Cider's Golden Touch

Apple cider, with its golden hue and natural sweetness, adds a delightful twist to the classic French apple cake. The Cider-Infused French Apple Cake celebrates the essence of autumn with the warm, comforting flavor of apple cider. It's a perfect dessert to savor on crisp, cool days when apples are at their peak.

This chapter explores how to make a delicious Cider-Infused French Apple Cake, highlighting the use of fresh apple cider for that authentic apple essence. Additionally, you'll discover techniques for creating a cider glaze that drizzles the cake with extra apple-infused goodness.

Recipe: Cider-Infused French Apple Cake

The Cider-Infused French Apple Cake is a delightful dessert that captures the essence of apple cider season. Here's the recipe:

Ingredients:

For the Cake:

- 3-4 medium-sized apples (a mix of sweet and tart varieties), peeled, cored, and diced
- 1 tablespoon lemon juice (to prevent apple browning)
- 1 1/2 cups all-purpose flour
- 1 1/2 teaspoons baking powder
- 1/2 teaspoon salt
- 1/2 cup unsalted butter, softened
- 1 cup granulated sugar
- 2 large eggs
- 1 teaspoon pure vanilla extract
- 1/4 cup fresh apple cider

For Using Fresh Apple Cider:

Tips on selecting and using fresh apple cider to infuse your cake with authentic apple flavor.

For Cider Glaze Techniques:

Step-by-step instructions on creating a cider glaze to drizzle over the cake, adding a layer of apple-infused sweetness.

Instructions:

For the Cake:

Preheat your oven to 350°F (175°C). Grease and flour a 9-inch (23 cm) round cake pan.

In a bowl, toss the diced apples with lemon juice to prevent browning. Set them aside.

In a separate bowl, whisk together the flour, baking powder, and salt.

In a large mixing bowl, cream the softened butter and granulated sugar together until light and fluffy, which takes about 2-3 minutes with an electric mixer.

Add the eggs, one at a time, beating well after each addition. Stir in the pure vanilla extract.

Gradually add the dry ingredients to the wet ingredients, mixing until just combined.

Stir in the fresh apple cider until you have a smooth batter.

Gently fold in the diced apples, ensuring they are evenly distributed throughout the batter.

For Using Fresh Apple Cider:

Select high-quality, fresh apple cider to infuse your cake with authentic apple flavor. Look for cider that's free from additives and preservatives.

Consider reducing the apple cider on the stovetop before adding it to the cake batter to intensify the cider flavor.

For Cider Glaze Techniques:

Create a cider glaze by combining fresh apple cider with powdered sugar. Adjust the proportions to achieve your desired consistency—thicker for a drizzle or thinner for a glaze.

Drizzle the cider glaze over the cooled cake, allowing it to drip down the sides for a sweet finish.

The Cider-Infused French Apple Cake is a delightful dessert that captures the essence of autumn with the warmth and sweetness of fresh apple cider. It's a wonderful way to celebrate the season's bountiful apple harvest and add a touch of coziness to your dessert table.

Chapter 18: Tips for Perfectly Caramelized Apples

Mastering Caramelization

Caramelized apples are a key ingredient in many French apple cake recipes, lending their rich, sweet flavor and tender texture to the dessert. However, achieving perfectly caramelized apples requires a few key techniques and tricks. In this chapter, we'll delve into the art of caramelization, exploring the nuances of selecting the right apples, mastering caramel techniques, and ensuring the storage of caramelized apples for your culinary creations.

Apple Selection for Caramelization

Choosing the right apples is crucial when it comes to caramelization. Here are some tips:

Variety Matters: opt for apples that maintain their shape and don't turn mushy when cooked. Varieties like Granny Smith, Honeycrisp, or Pink Lady work well due to their crisp texture.

Balance of Sweet and Tart: A combination of sweet and tart apples can provide a well-rounded flavor profile in your caramelized apples.

Caramel Tricks and Techniques

Mastering the caramelization process is essential for creating that rich, sweet flavor in your apples. Consider the following techniques:

Even Slicing: Slice your apples evenly to ensure they cook uniformly. Thinner slices will caramelize faster.

Butter and Sugar: Use a combination of butter and sugar in the pan. The butter adds flavor, while the sugar contributes to caramelization.

Low and Slow: Start caramelization over low to medium-low heat to avoid burning the sugar. Patience is key; rushing can result in burnt caramel.

Stirring and Patience: Stir the apples occasionally to ensure even caramelization. It's normal for the apples to release some moisture before the caramelization process begins.

Deglazing: If you notice the sugar starting to crystallize, you can deglaze the pan with a small amount of water to dissolve the sugar and prevent it from becoming grainy.

Caramelized Apple Storage Tips

If you have leftover caramelized apples or want to prepare them in advance, here are some storage tips:

Refrigeration: Caramelized apples can be stored in an airtight container in the refrigerator for up to 3-4 days. Be sure to let them cool completely before refrigerating.

Freezing: For longer storage, caramelized apples can be frozen in a freezer-safe container for up to 2-3 months. Thaw them in the refrigerator before using.

Reheating: To revive the flavors and textures of refrigerated or frozen caramelized apples, gently reheat them in a saucepan over low heat. Add a splash of water or apple juice to prevent them from drying out.

Mastering the art of caramelized apples is a valuable skill for creating delicious French apple cakes and a variety of other desserts. With the right apple selection and careful attention to caramelization techniques, you can ensure that your caramelized apples are a perfect addition to your culinary creations.

Chapter 19: Serving Suggestions and Pairings

Plating and Presentation Ideas

The art of serving a French apple cake extends beyond the taste alone; it's about creating a visual and sensory experience for your guests. In this chapter, we'll explore creative plating and presentation ideas that elevate your French apple cake from a delicious dessert to a work of culinary art.

Beverage Pairings

Choosing the right beverage to accompany your French apple cake can enhance the overall dining experience. Whether you prefer tea, coffee, or something a bit more indulgent, we'll explore beverage pairings that complement the flavors of your cake.

French Apple Cake Variations

Variety is the spice of life, and the world of French apple cakes offers numerous possibilities for experimentation. In this section, we'll delve into variations of the classic French apple cake, exploring unique flavors, ingredients, and textures to inspire your baking adventures.

Entertaining with Elegance

Hosting a gathering or dinner party? French apple cake can be the centerpiece of an elegant dessert table. We'll provide tips and ideas for entertaining with grace and style, making your French apple cake the star of the show.

From plating your cake like a Michelin-starred dessert to discovering the perfect wine or tea to accompany It.

Chapter 20: Mastering French Apple Cake Baking Techniques

Expert Baking Tips

Mastering the art of French apple cake involves honing your baking skills to create a dessert that's not only delicious but also visually stunning. In this chapter, we'll explore expert baking tips that will elevate your French apple cake from good to exceptional.

Ingredient Selection:

Apples: Choose a mix of sweet and tart apple varieties for a balanced flavor. Experiment with different types to discover unique flavor profiles.

Flour: Use high-quality all-purpose flour or a gluten-free blend, depending on dietary preferences. Sift the flour to ensure a smoother batter.

Butter: opt for unsalted butter to control the salt content in your cake. Ensure it's at room temperature for even mixing.

Eggs: Use fresh, large eggs. Let them come to room temperature before incorporating them into the batter.

Spices: Experiment with spices like cinnamon, nutmeg, or cardamom to add depth to your cake's flavor.

Precise Techniques:

Measuring Ingredients: Invest in a digital kitchen scale for precise ingredient measurements. Baking is a science, and accuracy matters.

Creaming Butter and Sugar: Cream the butter and sugar together until light and fluffy. This step incorporates air into the batter, resulting in a tender cake.

Uniform Apple Slices: Slice the apples uniformly to ensure even cooking. Use a mandoline slicer or a sharp knife for consistent thickness.

Folding Technique: When folding in the apples, use a gentle, folding motion to prevent overmixing and maintain the cake's texture.

Troubleshooting Common Issues

Even experienced bakers encounter challenges in the kitchen. Here are solutions to common French apple cake baking problems:

Soggy Bottom Crust: Pre-bake the crust for a few minutes to create a barrier that prevents moisture from the apples from making the crust soggy.

Apple Floatation: Toss apple slices in a bit of flour or cornstarch before adding them to the batter to help them distribute evenly throughout the cake.

Uneven Apple Distribution: Arrange apple slices evenly in the batter and press them slightly to ensure they're well-incorporated.

Perfecting the French Apple Cake

Creating the perfect French apple cake involves attention to detail and a deep understanding of the ingredients and techniques. Here's how to perfect your French apple cake:

Consistency: Aim for a cake that's moist but not wet. Adjust the amount of liquid and baking time accordingly.

Flavor Balance: Taste your apples to gauge their sweetness and adjust the sugar accordingly. Balance the sweetness with the tartness of the apples.

Texture: Achieve the perfect texture by not overmixing the batter. Fold gently to maintain a tender crumb.

Advanced Decorating Technique

For those looking to take their French apple cake to the next level, here's an advanced decorating technique that will impress even the most discerning dessert enthusiasts:

Fondant Apple Roses:

Create delicate apple-shaped fondant roses to adorn your French apple cake. Roll out red and green fondant, cut into petal shapes, and assemble them into lifelike roses. Place these edible works of art on your cake for a stunning presentation.

By delving into the finer points of French apple cake baking, you'll become a true master of this classic dessert. Whether you're a seasoned baker or just starting your culinary journey, this chapter offers valuable insights to help you achieve baking excellence.

Thank you.